Tom,

Steve and Linda tell us you love learning, love books, and that you are relatively new to Texas. So, enjoy this book and learn about the beauty of Texas wildlife.

Happy Birthday!

Gary Clark
Kathy Adams Clark
Mar 2005

TEXAS WILDLIFE
Portfolio

Photography by **KAC Productions**
and **Dave Welling**

Text by **Gary Clark**

ABOVE: Long-billed thrasher. DAVE WELLING

RIGHT: Yellow mud turtle. GLENN HAYES / KAC PRODUCTIONS

TITLE PAGE: Nine-banded armadillo. GREG LASLEY / KAC PRODUCTIONS

FRONT COVER: Little blue heron. Dave Welling

BACK COVER: Northern Bullock's oriole. DAVE WELLING
Baby opossum. LARRY DITTO / KAC PRODUCTIONS
Coyotes. DAVE WELLING

FRONT FLAP: Kemp's ridley sea turtle. LARRY DITTO / KAC PRODUCTIONS

ISBN 1-56037-260-5

© 2004 Farcountry Press

Photographs © 2004 KAC Productions and Dave Welling

Text by Gary Clark

For more information on our books write Farcountry Press, P.O. Box 5630, Helena, MT 59604; call (800) 821-3874; or visit www.farcountrypress.com

Created, produced, and designed in the United States.

Printed in Korea.

Foreword

Texans talk about Texas in grandiloquent terms. The biggest this, the biggest that, and so on. Most of the talk is overly prideful. But when it comes to talking about Texas wildlife, Texans have every right to be grandiloquent.

Texas leads all other states in bird diversity, with 622 species clearly documented for the state, including the extinct passenger pigeon and Carolina parakeet. During the annual National Audubon Society's Christmas Bird Counts, some Texas coastal regions tally over 200 species of birds, with the Mad Island Marsh count near Bay City leading the nation with over 230 species.

Vying with California and New Mexico for the most species of terrestrial mammals, Texas has over 140 species. Add marine mammals and the Texas list grows to about 181.

Reptiles and amphibians probably put Texas in first place for numbers of those species. An astonishing array of 73 species of reptiles and 21 species of amphibians reside in the state, including the American alligator, 50 species of lizards, 76 species of snakes, and 29 species of terrestrial and sea turtles.

Of course, comparison of wildlife numbers among states is tricky, subject to debate, and a bit silly since wild animals are oblivious to state boundaries. Every state has wonderful varieties of wildlife. Texas has a unique bounty of wildlife because of a unique landscape.

Texas is, after all, a big state with a big landscape. Still, the bigness of the land doesn't draw wildlife; rather, the diversity of the land gives Texas its abundance of wild creatures. This is a land with mountains rising out of desert plains, vast stretches of pine forests, 624 miles of coastline, long rivers and streams, semi-tropical thickets along the lower Rio Grande, gentle limestone hillsides, and grassland prairies that roll across high plains.

Altogether, Texas has eleven natural regions. These distinct environments attract wildlife as diverse as pronghorn antelope in West Texas and Kemp's ridley sea turtles on the Gulf Coast. Prairie dogs live in the Panhandle plains, southern flying squirrels in the eastern forests, and green jays in the Rio Grande delta.

Yet, much of the Texas landscape and its wildlife have changed since the founding of the sovereign Republic of Texas in 1836. Back then, the region was largely prairie

This great egret is in high breeding plumage, as indicated by the green lores. It is perched on a tallow tree at the famous rookery in the Houston Audubon Society's High Island Bird Sanctuary. Great egrets, unlike the invasive tallow trees, are indigenous to the wetlands of Texas.
GREG LASLEY / KAC PRODUCTIONS

grassland hosting untold multitudes of bison from the Panhandle to the Mexican border. A huge portion of East Texas comprised the Big Thicket, a dense wilderness of pines and hardwoods, where clouds of passenger pigeons moved through in October. The Chihuahuan Desert with its rugged mountains in south-western Texas was a land replete with mountain lions and golden eagles. And the Rio Grande rushed wide and wild from El Paso to Brownsville with egrets and muskrats common in its waters.

All that has changed. Invasive plants, agriculture, urbanization, and dams have altered prairies, lev-eled forests, and dried up 250 miles of the Rio Grande from El Paso to Presidio. Bison are all but gone from Texas, passenger pigeons are extinct, and mountain lions are rare.

Despite alterations of the land, wildlife is still plentiful. Waterfowl such as ducks, geese, and sandhill cranes arrive in the winter by the millions on the coastal plain; white-tailed deer are abundant through-out the state, coyotes roam every-where, and pronghorn antelope graze on the high plains.

Tens of thousands of migratory songbirds and shorebirds travel from the tropics through Texas every

the Colima warbler. Bird watchers from all over the world hike the rugged mountain slopes just to get a glimpse of the bird.

Texas is still a land of adventure for people who love to see wildlife. With 120 state parks, 51 wildlife management areas, 13 national wildlife refuges, 13 national parks and historic sites (most having wildlife areas,) 4 national forests, 5 national grasslands, and scores of county parks, Texas offers many opportunities to see its variety of wild creatures.

Nature photographers love Texas. Opportunities to get extraordinary wildlife photographs are almost limitless. And the chances to add diverse images of wildlife to a photographic portfo-lio make Texas a magnet for nature photographers.

The photographs in this book were taken by nine highly experi-enced nature photographers. Eight of these photographers are Texas residents represented by KAC Productions, a stock agency based in The Woodlands, Texas. Those photographers are Kathy Adams Clark (owner of KAC Productions), Larry Ditto, Bill Draker, Glenn Hayes, Greg Lasley, Rolf Nussbaumer, and John and Gloria Tveten.

spring on their way to breeding grounds farther north. Many of these birds nest in Texas, but whatever the case, migratory birds make Texas a world hotspot for bird watchers.

The awe-inspiring western wilderness terrain of Big Bend National Park and Big Bend Ranch State Park forms the nation's last frontier. There, black bears, mountain lions, jackrabbits, and umpteen kinds of lizards live in virtual isolation from modern civilization.

The Chisos Mountains of Big Bend National Park are the only place in North America to find breeding pairs of a little Mexican bird called

The ninth person is Dave Welling, a California resident and well-known nature photographer who has spent much of his time and energy focusing his camera on Texas wildlife.

All the photographers have spent many hours hiking trails, traveling back roads, crouching in photography blinds, and studying the lives of wildlife in order to create the captivating images on the pages of this book. Their photographs show why Texans may wax grandiloquently about Texas wildlife.

—Gary Clark

ABOVE: Collared peccaries, or "javelinas," occupy the arid regions of Texas where prickly pear cacti are abundant. Peccary families bed down in dense areas of prickly pear during the heat of the day. At dawn and dusk they come out in the open to feed on mesquite beans, cacti, and other succulent vegetation. DAVE WELLING

FACING PAGE: Foxes are members of the canine family, which includes dogs, coyotes, and wolves. Unlike other canines, foxes have yellow eyes with elliptical, catlike pupils. Their eyes equip them for nocturnal hunting.

Foxes have other characteristics similar to cats. They are stealthy and silent as they sneak through woods and fields. Fox tracks even have a gait similar to cats, with paw prints that run in a straight line, front and hind prints that overlap, and claw prints that are barely detectable because of semi-retractable claws. GREG LASLEY / KAC PRODUCTIONS

ABOVE: *The mockingbird can reproduce the songs of at least thirty-six other bird species. In addition, it can replicate the sounds of frogs, dogs, pianos, wind chimes, doorbells, and cellular phones and can combine such sounds into complex harmonies of 200 distinct songs.*

Mockingbirds are aggressive defenders of their territories. A folk tale claims that when Texas legislators adopted the mockingbird as the state bird in 1927, they wrote a resolution describing the bird as "a fighter for the protection of his home, falling, if need be, in its defense, like any true Texan…." DAVE WELLING

LEFT: *Among the most abundant of Texas mammals, the sleek and swift-footed white-tailed deer ranges throughout Texas in any habitat with dense woody cover or grass cover. They are most active in the early morning and late afternoon and often graze in the grass along roadsides.* DAVE WELLING

ABOVE: Painted buntings migrate to Texas in the spring from Mexico and Panama. Although common in spring and summer, painted buntings are somewhat secretive and often hard to find. The rainbow-colored male can best be seen at sunrise when he perches high on a branch to sing.

Despite having an appetite for seed, painted buntings seldom visit backyard birdfeeders where seed is plentiful. They are shy of open, exposed places. ROLF NUSSBAUMER / KAC PRODUCTIONS

FACING PAGE: Found throughout Texas, coyotes have a distinct doglike appearance. DAVE WELLING

ABOVE: *Several species of bats make Texas their home. The eastern pipistrelles in this photograph occupy the eastern two-thirds of the state from the Panhandle to South Texas. On an early summer evening, it is possible to see them fluttering mothlike along waterways and over pastures.* JOHN & GLORIA TVETEN / KAC PRODUCTIONS

LEFT: *Alligators live in freshwater swamps and marshes as well as in creeks and small lakes. They keep wetlands healthy by consuming rodents such as nutrias that would otherwise overgraze wetland vegetation.* LARRY DITTO / KAC PRODUCTIONS

RIGHT: The southern flying squirrel, with soft gray-brown fur, will fit in the palm of one's hand. Though seldom seen, it is quite common in neighborhoods containing oak and pine trees in the eastern third of the state. It doesn't really fly but instead sails from tree trunk to tree trunk on flaps of skin stretched between its front and back legs. When clinging to a tree trunk, the squirrel becomes virtually invisible because of its miniature size and cryptic coloration.
JOHN & GLORIA TVETEN / KAC PRODUCTIONS

BELOW: The western diamondback rattlesnake is a member of the venomous pit viper family of snakes. It is a nocturnal creature that spends the day coiled in the shade of a bush or under a rock to keep from overheating in the sun.
BILL DRAKER / KAC PRODUCTIONS

Modest numbers of Cooper's hawks are present in Texas year round and become somewhat more numerous in winter when migrant populations arrive. The birds are not common breeders in Texas. They are in the Accipiter genus of raptors and are expanding their habitat from forests and thornbrush into city parks, wooded neighborhoods, and tree-lined golf courses. This young bird is wet after a morning bath. DAVE WELLING

ABOVE: The flamboyant and resplendent green jay is a permanent resident of the Rio Grande Valley in South Texas. DAVE WELLING

RIGHT: Rio Grande leopard frogs occupy ponds, creeks, and cattle tanks in the arid regions of Texas. DAVE WELLING

A large colony of Neotropical cormorants roosting at sunset. LARRY DITTO / KAC PRODUCTIONS

The western screech-owl lives in scattered locations in the western part of Texas. The best places to find it are in Big Bend National Park and the Davis Mountains. GREG LASLEY / KAC PRODUCTIONS

Cooper's hawk. Cooper's hawks and sharp-shinned hawks are similar in appearance; each has a 2-foot wingspan, long tail, and reddish barring on the breast. One difference between the two hawks is the squared-off tail-tip of the sharp-shinned and the rounded tail-tip of the Cooper's. But an easier and surer distinguishing characteristic is their flight profiles—the head of the Cooper's hawk protrudes beyond the leading line of the wings and the sharp-shinned's head is on an even plane with the wing line.

Both hawks are fast, agile, and stealthy predators. They take off quickly from a perch to attack prey such as mice, squirrels, songbirds, and, in the Southwest, reptiles. Many a backyard bird watcher has seen a sharp-shinned hawk suddenly swoop down to a birdfeeder and snatch a cardinal, chickadee, or squirrel in its talons. DAVE WELLING

LEFT: *Residing only in the Trans-Pecos region of Big Bend and adjacent counties of Texas, the hooded skunk is a secretive creature. It ambles quietly across the ground searching for insects, small rodents, and prickly pear fruit.* DAVE WELLING

BELOW: *Hispid cotton rats inhabit areas where they can scurry under protective tall grasses such as bluestem and cordgrass. The little mammals are favored food for hawks, owls, coyotes, and snakes.* DAVE WELLING

RIGHT: Armadillos hang out around water holes on hot summer days. Like pigs, they drink and wallow in the water to cool off.
DAVE WELLING

BELOW: The gangly grove-billed ani in South Texas gets its name from the grooves in the robust culmen of its bill.
BILL DRAKER / KAC PRODUCTIONS

FAR RIGHT: Gray foxes look like overgrown cats at about 3 feet in length and weighing between 7 and 13 pounds. Their coarse, gray hair has a salt-and-pepper appearance due to the mixture of black-and-white bands in their guard hairs. Their bellies are an iron-red color, and they have a long, bushy, ruddy-gray tail with a black tip and a black stripe running vertically down the top.

A gray fox may build a den in the hollow of a tree 10 feet off the ground. It is the only member of the dog family in North America that can climb trees—hence its nickname, tree fox. GREG LASLEY / KAC PRODUCTIONS

LEFT: A southwestern cousin and look-alike of the northern cardinal, the pyrrhuloxia not surprisingly has the folk name "Texas cardinal."
DAVE WELLING

FACING PAGE: The "points" on the antlers of a white-tailed buck are not a reliable indicator of age because antler growth is more dependent on adequate nutrition than on longevity. Older bucks, though, may have heavier bases on their antlers than younger bucks.
GLENN HAYES / KAC PRODUCTIONS

RIGHT: The orange-crowned warbler is a common spring migrant in the state. Small numbers can be found in the winter throughout Texas except in the Panhandle. In this photograph, the orange-colored crown of a breeding-plumaged bird is visible as the bird bathes in a pool of water. DAVE WELLING

BELOW: Imported from South America for the fur trade, nutrias are now a prevalent nuisance in waterways, ponds, and lakes in the eastern two-thirds of Texas. The overpopulation of these herbivores has wreaked havoc in lakes and marshes statewide.
KATHY ADAMS CLARK / KAC PRODUCTIONS

FACING PAGE: The bobcat stands 2 feet tall and weighs 15 to 30 pounds, about the size of a medium-sized dog. Most active at night, bobcats often prowl along streams or across fields just before sunset. DAVE WELLING

ABOVE: The Texas tortoise ranges from south-central Texas to the Mexican states of Coahuila, Tamaulipas, and Nuevo León. Primarily a vegetarian, the tortoise feeds on the fruit of prickly pears and other succulent vegetation. DAVE WELLING

FACING PAGE: Black-necked stilts occupy a variety of locations throughout the state except in the forested regions of East Texas. In courtship display, the male preens his feathers, pecks the water or ground in front of a female, walks around her flicking water with his beak, and finally mounts her to mate. DAVE WELLING

ABOVE: Often called the Mexican eagle, the crested caracara is not akin to eagles but is instead related to falcons. It occupies the prairie lands and farm fields of Texas, competing with vultures for carrion and running through grassy fields to capture live prey such as snakes and rats. DAVE WELLING

FACING PAGE: This is a white-tailed buck in the fall, when mating is the animal's primary concern. The velvet has been shed from its antlers and the neck muscles have thickened, readying it to compete with other males for dominance of the females. GLEN HAYES / KAC PRODUCTIONS

ABOVE: *A great blue heron will stand statuesque or wade in slow motion through shallow water waiting for an opportunity to spear frogs, snakes, and fish with its swordlike beak. Great blues can stab prey with an accuracy that would be the envy of any fencing master.* DAVE WELLING

FACING PAGE: *American alligator adults can measure 6 to 14 feet long and weigh 500 pounds. They date back 65 to 100 million years when dinosaurs roamed the earth. However, alligators are not a species of dinosaur no matter how much they might look like one.* DAVE WELLING

RIGHT: The barn owl is a large, tawny owl with a white, heart-shaped facial disk. It feeds mostly on rodents such as mice or ground birds such as quail.

When this photo was taken, the owl was bobbing, weaving, and hissing in an attempt to scare away an intruder. BILL DRAKER / KAC PRODUCTIONS

BELOW: Fox squirrels get their name from the ruddy, foxlike fur that adorns their plump bodies. The underbelly has a yellowish cast and the tail is cinnamon colored. Fox squirrels roam the eastern two-thirds of Texas and favor open, upland forests. GLENN HAYES / KAC PRODUCTIONS

ABOVE: The Kemp's ridley sea turtle is the smallest of all sea turtles. When the baby in this photograph matures, it will weigh about 100 pounds and grow to 3 feet in length. Kemp's is a graceful sea creature, sailing the sea with a heart-shaped, olive-green carapace that looks like sculpted marble.

Kemp's ridley sea turtles disappeared from Texas beaches in the mid-twentieth century. In a desperate effort to restore the turtles to Texas, people gathered eggs at Rancho Nuevo, Mexico, and placed them in the sand at Padre Island National Seashore. The theory behind that endeavor was that Kemp's imprint on their natal beaches and return to the beaches to nest. The theory proved true, and in 2003 thirty-seven Kemp's nested on Texas beaches. LARRY DITTO / KAC PRODUCTIONS

FACING PAGE: The black-bellied whistling-duck ranges from the lower two-thirds of the Texas coast to the coasts of Mexico and Central America. This handsome bird's high-pitched whistling notes echo over shallow lakes and freshwater marshes. DAVE WELLING

ABOVE: Research conducted by Texas A&M University scientists indicates that lesser sandhill cranes, a subspecies of sandhill cranes, breed during the summer in Siberia and travel 7,000 miles to spend the winter in the Panhandle of Texas. GLENN HAYES / KAC PRODUCTIONS

RIGHT: Even though folk-named "prairie wolf," coyotes are not restricted to prairies. They inhabit woods, beaches, and even urban neighborhoods. LARRY DITTO / KAC PRODUCTIONS

The Texas spiny lizard is usually seen on trees, especially mesquite, but can also be found on wooden fence posts and walls. The Texas spiny lizard ranges from the Red River in North Texas down to northern Mexico.
DAVE WELLING

LEFT: The green kingfisher is seen uncommonly in Central and South Texas and along the Rio Grande from Brownsville to the Pecos River. It hunts from a height of 3 to 6 feet above shallow water. LARRY DITTO / KAC PRODUCTIONS

BELOW: A male northern bobwhite feeds in a grassy field. Bobwhites can be found throughout Texas except in the far western part of the state. For a variety of reasons, including climate change and loss of habitat, populations of bobwhites in Texas are diminishing. DAVE WELLING

LEFT: The white-tipped dove of the Rio Grande Valley is a plump dove that has a celestial white forehead with white tips on the outer edges of the tail. It makes a low-pitched, hollow-sounding "hoo-hoo-hoo" call, like the sound of a child blowing air across the opening of an empty bottle.

The dove has long symbolized values of peace and virtue. In the biblical story of the flood, a dove sent out by Noah from the ark returned with an olive branch, signifying that the waters were receding and that God had made peace with humankind. Of the four cardinal virtues in medieval Christendom—prudence, justice, temperance, and fortitude—the dove symbolized temperance. BILL DRAKER / KAC PRODUCTIONS

RIGHT: Among nature's most elegant animals is the pronghorn antelope, which is not really an antelope but the sole surviving member of an ancient mammalian family called Antilocapra that dates back 60 million years. Pronghorns once roamed in huge herds throughout West Texas but today are limited to small herds in the Trans-Pecos and Panhandle regions.

It is common to be startled by the appearance of pronghorns on a West Texas high plain. That's because pronghorns have sleek, deerlike bodies with brown backs and white flanks that make them nearly invisible on the high plains. Early cowboys called them "prairie ghosts."

Pronghorns are the fastest mammal in North America, reaching speeds of 60 miles per hour. Meriwether Lewis of the famed Lewis and Clark Expedition wrote in his journal that running pronghorns "appeared reather the rappid flight of birds than the motion of quadrupeds." JOHN & GLORIA TVETEN / KAC PRODUCTIONS

RIGHT: The scissor-tailed flycatcher migrates to Texas from Mexico and Panama in the spring to breed. It is a lovely, graceful bird known as the Texas bird of paradise. The long, forked tail that opens and closes like a pair of scissors helps enable this acrobatic bird to snare insects on the wing.
BILL DRAKER / KAC PRODUCTIONS

BELOW: Common pauraques reside in the woodlands of southern Texas. If flushed, they fly along the ground at an altitude rarely exceeding 10 feet. DAVE WELLING

FACING PAGE: Raccoons look like Zorro with their black masks; and as was Zorro, they are stealthy and smart. They can pry the lids off garbage cans and pick seeds out of birdfeeders. They eat seeds, berries, carrion, rodents, insects, frogs, and small fish. LARRY DITTO / KAC PRODUCTIONS

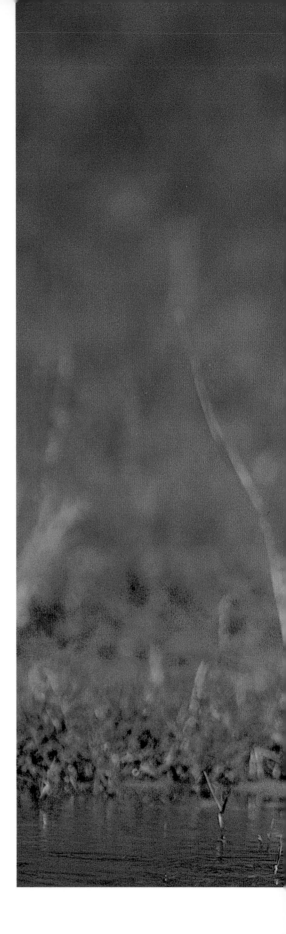

RIGHT: A leopard frog in a shallow freshwater marsh is a quick meal for the great blue heron. DAVE WELLING

BELOW: Rat snakes are sometimes called "chicken snakes" because they lurk around chicken coops. Actually, they don't normally feed on chickens or baby chicks but on rodents that live around the chicken yard. Rat snakes also slither up low trees and shrubs in search of rodents and small bird eggs. DAVE WELLING

RIGHT: *Hardly noticeable to the human eye, the sora resides in dense marshes, swamps, and other wetlands in Texas. The 8-inch-long bird of the rail family hunts for seeds and insects in the mud and shallow water.* LARRY DITTO / KAC PRODUCTIONS

BELOW: *White-tailed deer in South Texas browsing on leaves.* DAVE WELLING

Baby swamp rabbits in a nest beneath a clump of tangled vines along the banks of a marsh.
JOHN & GLORIA TVETEN / KAC PRODUCTIONS

The greater roadrunner ranges throughout Texas except in the extreme coastal marshes along the Louisiana border. It is common along roadways and in open fields in the western and southern part of the state. ROLF NUSSBAUMER / KAC PRODUCTIONS

RIGHT: To escape the heat of the day, Rio Grande leopard frogs rest in shade under a rocky ledge along a pool of water. DAVE WELLING

BELOW: A female northern shoveler with her distinctive spatula-shaped beak. BILL DRAKER / KAC PRODUCTIONS

FAR RIGHT: Despite menacing facial expressions and frightful grunting noises, collared peccaries are usually harmless to humans and livestock. The relatively passive animals are herbivores that travel in small herds at dawn and dusk, feeding rather voraciously on prickly pear cacti. DAVE WELLING

RIGHT: One of the prettier non-venomous snakes of West Texas, the Texas longnose snake has alternating red and black patches on its back and splotchy cream-colored tones on its sides. The red patches vary from a pinkish-rose color in Big Bend country to a reddish-orange color in Panhandle country. A clever defense of the Texas longnose snake is to exude blood from its cloaca and writhe violently. DAVE WELLING

BELOW: The belted kingfisher is the only kingfisher that ranges throughout Texas. It plunges in a steep dive into open water from an overhanging limb or power line to capture a fish. DAVE WELLING

Coyotes are opportunistic feeders, devouring nearly any source of food. This coyote is feeding on a wild pig killed by a landowner.
GREG LASLEY /
KAC PRODUCTIONS

A white-tailed buck silhouetted against the setting sun.
BILL DRAKER /
KAC PRODUCTIONS

The Bullock's oriole is a summer resident of the western half of Texas, where it nests in open woodlands. ROLF NUSSBAUMER / KAC PRODUCTIONS

A javelina scratches itself by the early morning light at a West Texas mud hole. DAVE WELLING

Curve-billed thrashers range from western Texas into southern Arizona and south into Mexico. They occupy arid locations where mesquite and other scrubby trees provide adequate protection and cover. DAVE WELLING

The Virginia opossum is North America's only marsupial. Its hind feet have four outer toes and an inner toe that acts like a human thumb. An opossum has a lustrous gray-white coat with an underbelly of soft, wool-like fur.

This baby is following its mother as she forages for scraps of fruit, grains, carrion, and—most important—roaches.

LARRY DITTO / KAC PRODUCTIONS

A pair of white-tailed bucks sparring at a water hole. DAVE WELLING

ABOVE: Green jays aggressively defend their feeding territory. When a human enters their territory, green jays approach the person and make a raucous sound to drive the intruder away. ROLF NUSSBAUMER / KAC PRODUCTIONS

FACING PAGE: Bobcats feed on small rodents, squirrels, and rabbits. They also attack small domestic farm animals such as chickens and goats but rarely decimate a barnyard of its livestock. Bobcats live throughout the state and often reside in close proximity to humans. GLENN HAYES / KAC PRODUCTIONS

LEFT: *The black-tailed prairie dog is no relative of the dog. Instead, it is a ground squirrel living in the shortgrass prairies of Texas.*
LARRY DITTO / KAC PRODUCTIONS

BELOW: *The shy coral snake is legendary for its venomous bite. The rhyme "red and yellow kill a fellow" lets Texans know when they've encountered a coral snake rather than a harmless milk snake.*
KATHY ADAMS CLARK / KAC PRODUCTIONS

FACING PAGE: *At 2 feet tall, the great horned owl is the largest of Texas owls. It hunts for rabbits, skunks, and opossums in both open spaces and wooded areas. The call is a resonating low-pitched "whoo-whoo-whoo."* ROLF NUSSBAUMER / KAC PRODUCTIONS

ABOVE: Blue mockingbirds, common in Mexico, had not been documented in Texas until May 1999. Since that time, they've appeared at several locations in the Rio Grande Valley, much to the delight of bird watchers there.
LARRY DITTO / KAC PRODUCTIONS

RIGHT: Mexican free-tailed bats flying from the Frio Bat Cave near Concan at twilight. The bats leave the cave at speeds up to 35 miles per hour and gobble up small moths caught on the wing.

The Frio Bat Cave is a maternity cave where pups are born in June and July. An estimated 10 million bats leave the cave each evening in August when mothers and pups fly out together to hunt. GREG LASLEY / KAC PRODUCTIONS

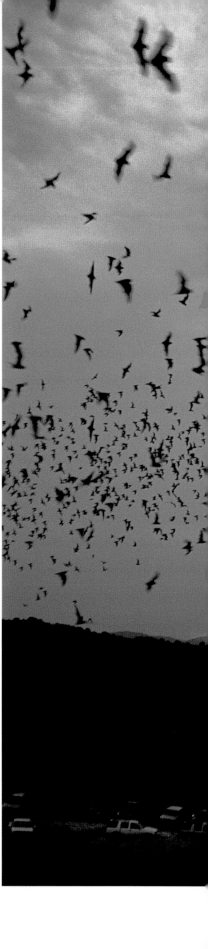

Early nineteenth-century surveyor Vernon Bailey estimated there were 800 million prairie dogs living on tens of thousands of acres in West Texas. One prairie dog "town" extended for 250 miles from San Angelo to Clarendon. The population of prairie dogs in Texas today has dwindled to 2 million.

The anhinga often swims with its body submerged and its neck above the water, making it appear as a "snake bird," which is an old folk name. Also known as "water turkey" because of a long black tail, anhingas breed in the eastern part of the state.

RIGHT: *Less than a foot long, the least bittern is a master of camouflage with cryptic coloration that blends with marsh vegetation. It steps lightly among the cattails of a shallow, freshwater marsh hunting for small fish, crawfish, and frogs.*
LARRY DITTO / KAC PRODUCTIONS

BELOW: *The swamp rabbit is the largest of the cottontail rabbits of Texas and has a white tail and coarse gray-brown fur tipped with black. Its fur is waterproof, which enables it to swim across bayous and even dive under water.* DAVE WELLING

A threatened species, the Texas horned lizard, known by its folk name "horny toad" with its horns and armored plating, is a docile and gentle creature. After warming its body in the morning sun, it spends the day feeding on harvester ants or just lounging in the sun. The Texas horned lizard is active only from April to October, spending the remainder of the year hibernating. LARRY DITTO / KAC PRODUCTIONS

ABOVE: The ringtailed cat has been variously named civit cat, mountain cat, and raccoon fox. It is a relative of the raccoon and, like the raccoon, is nocturnal. Sightings of the critter are rare even though it ranges throughout the state.
DAVE WELLING

LEFT: Ospreys soar on 6-foot wingspans in wide circles over a body of water, hover momentarily, and then suddenly plunge feet first into the water to grab a fish in their sharp talons. Ospreys catch a fish in eight out of ten attempts, the envy of any human angler.

Ospreys are unmistakable in flight because of their angled wings that crook backward at the elbow. Their white-capped heads, white bellies, and white underwing linings contrast dramatically with the rich, chocolate-brown feathering on the back.
DAVE WELLING

ABOVE: American alligator babies emerge from the nest in late summer. The adult female is always close to her young, fiercely protecting them from predators like skunks, humans, and even adult male alligators.
LARRY DITTO / KAC PRODUCTIONS

FACING PAGE: The purple gallinule takes the prize as the most beautiful bird of Texas summers. Its striking purple and blue feathers, blue forehead shield, and yellow-tipped red bill make it unmistakable in freshwater marshes in the eastern part of the state. LARRY DITTO / KAC PRODUCTIONS

This white-tailed buck is browsing on leaves. Deer browse on trees and graze on grasses.
GLENN HAYES / KAC PRODUCTIONS

RIGHT: John James Audubon named the Bewick's wren in honor of his friend Thomas Bewick, an English engraver who wrote and illustrated a book on British birds. DAVE WELLING

BELOW: Mexican ground squirrels are found throughout the western and southern parts of Texas. Their burrows are important to desert ecology because they provide shelter for salamanders, lizards, and other animals.

The diminutive, delicate-looking squirrels have a natural resistance to the venom of western diamondback rattlesnakes. DAVE WELLING

*A handsome male
Bullock's oriole
bathing in a West
Texas water hole.*
DAVE WELLING

Northern pintail and mottled ducks on a coastal pond at sunset. LARRY DITTO / KAC PRODUCTIONS

Adult sandhill cranes stand 3 to 4 feet tall and have a wingspan of up to 7 feet.
DAVE WELLING

LEFT: *A baby great horned owl fluffing its downy feathers to scare off an intruder.* BILL DRAKER / KAC PRODUCTIONS

BELOW: *Mule deer range in the Trans-Pecos and Panhandle regions of Texas. Some have been introduced to other regions for hunting. Mule deer have a bounding gait that allows them to travel over the rocky West Texas landscape of thornbrush and cactus.* LARRY DITTO / KAC PRODUCTIONS

The incisors on nutrias are orange-colored. GREG LASLEY / KAC PRODUCTIONS

LEFT: *A western diamondback rattlesnake rears its head in an S-curve and vibrates its tail rattle as a warning to potential predators. The rattles are remnants of keratin from shed skin. The pits on the face of the rattlesnake act as heat sensors, which enable the snake to detect with deadly accuracy warm-blooded animals such as mice and rabbits. The snake can strike its victims at a distance of half its body length.*

Venom is the snake's most powerful weapon. A complex mixture of enzymes, venom quickly degrades nerve cells, fleshy tissue, muscle tissue, blood plasma, and the cardiovascular system. Rattlesnakes do not inject their deadly venom without a reason, because it takes them four days to replenish spent venom. DAVE WELLING

BELOW: *The Attwater's prairie chicken is struggling against extinction on the remnants of Texas coastal prairies. Less than fifty of these birds still exist in the wild, with about thirty on the Texas City Prairie Preserve and another eighteen on the Attwater Prairie Chicken National Wildlife Refuge near Eagle Lake. A little over a hundred years ago, more than a million of these birds roamed on 6 million acres of coastal prairie in Texas and Louisiana. As the coastal prairies dwindled to a small fraction of the landscape, the prairie chicken population all but disappeared.*

In the early morning hours from February through April, the male prairie chickens assemble on a grass flat called a lek. At dawn they begin strutting across the lek, stomping their feet, raising their tail feathers, and erecting blackish-orange neck feathers that look like horns above their head. They puff up bright golden air sacs on their necks and make a low-pitched "wooo-looo" sound resembling the timbre of kettledrums. KATHY ADAMS CLARK / KAC PRODUCTIONS

ABOVE: Although some ospreys stay in Texas all year, most migrate to the state from Alaska and Canada to spend the winter, and many travel to Mexico and Central America. The southern part of the state and coastal regions are the best places to find ospreys. GREG LASLEY / KAC PRODUCTIONS

LEFT: Redhead ducks, and other diving ducks in the genus Aythya, arrive for the winter in bays, coastal marshes, ponds, and freshwater lakes throughout Texas.

Seven of the eleven genera of North American diving ducks regularly show up in the coastal areas. The genus Aythya includes the majority of diving ducks such as canvasback, redhead, ring-necked, lesser scaup, and greater scaup. LARRY DITTO / KAC PRODUCTIONS

Few birds attract attention like a bald eagle. An adult bird is 3 feet long from head to tail, has a wingspan of 7 to 8 feet, and weighs 10 to 14 pounds.

Southern bald eagles breed from Florida to East Texas in the winter months. During their summer non-breeding cycle, these eagles travel northward to the Mississippi River Valley or go as far north as Montana across to New York.

The bald eagle's scientific name, Haliaeetus leuco-cephalus, literally means "sea eagle with a white head." The word "bald" in the English name derives from an archaic word meaning "shiny white." The bald eagle is the only species of sea eagle native to North America.

KATHY ADAMS CLARK / KAC PRODUCTIONS

RIGHT: Non-venomous bullsnakes are docile creatures that can put on an aggressive act. They posture like rattlesnakes, forming an S-curve as if ready to strike. They are found throughout Texas except in the extreme eastern and western parts of the state. DAVE WELLING

BELOW: A yellow mud turtle yawning in the mid-day sun. DAVE WELLING

ABOVE: Being reptiles, alligators are cold-blooded creatures that must depend on the ambient temperature to warm their bodies. The blood that runs through the thick skin of an alligator transfers heat collected from sunlight to the entire body. That's why alligators spend much of the day basking in the sun—they're not lazy, they're just warming up. KATHY ADAMS CLARK / KAC PRODUCTIONS

LEFT: The arrival of sandhill cranes in Texas is a sign of winter. Large numbers of sandhills spend the season around the lakes and cultivated fields in the western and southern parts of the state. BILL DRAKER / KAC PRODUCTIONS

LEFT: *The plains pocket mouse is a silky little creature of the Panhandle high plains. It burrows under a bush in sandy soil with sparse vegetation, and during the day it plugs the opening to the burrow to protect its home from predators.* JOHN & GLORIA TVETEN / KAC PRODUCTIONS

BELOW: *A common resident of South Texas Brush Country and the Trans-Pecos region, the Harris's hawk dives into brush in pursuit of rodents, squirrels, large insects, or small birds. Harris's hawks are used by falconers because they are cooperative and feed on a variety of mammals, reptiles, and amphibians.* DAVE WELLING

FACING PAGE: *Pronghorns live in open country. Although agile and fleet-footed, they are reluctant to jump a fence. They prefer to crawl under a fence or squeeze between the wires.* LARRY DITTO / KAC PRODUCTIONS

ABOVE: The black-tailed jackrabbit is Texas's only hare, and it can run at speeds up to 45 miles per hour. It is a big, 2-foot tall, lanky creature with yellow eyes and donkey-style ears as long as its hind legs. It has buff, pepper-colored fur above and dull whitish fur underneath. DAVE WELLING

RIGHT: At daybreak, sandhill cranes lift off and fly to nearby cultivated fields to feed on grain, berries, lizards, frogs, and snakes. GLENN HAYES / KAC PRODUCTIONS

LEFT: *Squirrels, like this fox squirrel, are in the mammal order Rodentia, akin to mice, rats, beavers, and nutrias. They have two pairs of incisors, one upper pair and one lower pair, but no canine teeth. The incisors grow continuously, which enables squirrels to gnaw away on a wooden birdfeeder and regrow their worn-down teeth without interrupting the gnawing.* KATHY ADAMS CLARK / KAC PRODUCTIONS

BELOW: *The Texas tortoise, with a carapace that measures 8 inches long, may live as long as sixty years. They reach sexual maturity by age fifteen. The Texas tortoise has been protected under the Endangered Species Act since 1977.* LARRY DITTO / KAC PRODUCTIONS

FACING PAGE: *Native birds of Africa, cattle egrets have had one of the more interesting odysseys in the bird world. No one knows why, but the birds somehow showed up in South America in the late nineteenth century, later to expand their range into the United States by the mid-twentieth century.*

Cattle egrets stand about 20 inches tall and often appear in association with cattle because of their inherited habit of following cloven-hoofed animals like water buffalo in Africa. Egrets feed on the insects stirred up by hoofed animals, but they also hunt in marshes for amphibians and small fish.

This breeding-plumaged bird is standing in a willow tree on the upper Texas coast. DAVE WELLING

American bison were misnamed "buffalo" by early European settlers because of the resemblance to the water buffalo of Africa and India. Bison are actually bovines, in the same family as cattle.

These majestic animals with mighty shoulders and shaggy fur once ranged across the North American Great Plains in herds so large that they blanketed prairie landscapes from horizon to horizon. Their populations were decimated by relentless and reckless hunting in the nineteenth century, today leaving only small herds on private or government-owned land.

KATHY ADAMS CLARK / KAC PRODUCTIONS

The eastern screech-owl is no bigger than an average soup can. Its beak protrudes slightly from behind a curtain of feathers, as opposed to the prominently visible beak of a hawk. As with most owls, the screech-owl has four toes—two pointing forward, one pointing backward, and one capable of rotating forward or backward to aid in snaring a mouse or securing a perch.

A ubiquitous owl in residential neighborhoods, the screech-owl feeds on insects, small rodents, lizards, and songbirds. DAVE WELLING

An Old World species in the family Suidae, feral hogs descend from a mixture of hogs including European hogs brought to North America 300 years ago, "Russian boars" brought over for hunting purposes in the 1930s, and escaped domestic pigs. Feral hogs are found primarily in the moist woodlands of East Texas, in the woodlands of Central Texas, and along the coastal plain into the Rio Grande Valley.

Feral hogs, known for their rapacious appetite for native vegetation and wildlife, are highly destructive to the land. LARRY DITTO / KAC PRODUCTIONS

LEFT: A black-and-white woodpecker with a handsome red crown and a face marked with black lines, the ladder-backed woodpecker is seen throughout Texas with the exception of the eastern Piney Woods. It feeds on insects in trees, cacti, and the ground. A male has a stout bill that allows it to dig deep into bark and cacti for insects. DAVE WELLING

BELOW: Black-bellied whistling-ducks form lifetime mating pairs that share all the duties of raising their young. LARRY DITTO / KAC PRODUCTIONS

Male turkeys, or toms, fan their iridescent tail feathers to impress females, or hens, in a mating display or to warn the flock of potential danger.
BILL DRAKER / KAC PRODUCTIONS

LEFT: *This greater roadrunner has fluffed its feathers and spread its wings to expose the underlying black skin to the warming rays of the morning sun.* DAVE WELLING

BELOW: *Virginia opossums live in every region of Texas except the extreme arid regions of the west.*

These babies are about two months old. When they were eleven or twelve days old and weighed only 1/5 of a gram, they crawled into their mother's pouch, attached themselves to a nipple, and fed until they were seven weeks old. JOHN & GLORIA TVETEN / KAC PRODUCTIONS

LEFT: *Formerly named solitary vireo, the 5-inch-long blue-headed vireo has a slate-blue head, white spectacles and throat, an olive back, and yellow flanks. It migrates during the spring through East Texas from Mexico and Central America as it heads to breeding grounds in the eastern United States and Canada.* LARRY DITTO / KAC PRODUCTIONS

BELOW: *Head to tail, this 6-inch-long keeled earless lizard has keels on the tiny scales covering its body. The male has large black bands on the side of his stomach. He does push-ups with his front legs when defending his territory or when trying to attract a female.*

Present only in dry, sandy places usually along the coast from southeastern Texas to northeastern Mexico, keeled earless lizards hunt for insects by day and burrow in the sand to keep warm at night. LARRY DITTO / KAC PRODUCTIONS

FACING PAGE: *Birds often get their names from their appearance, such as the roseate spoonbill, which is named for its deep pinkish color and flattened, spatula-shaped bill.* DAVE WELLING

ABOVE: *Mountain bluebirds nest in the western half of the United States.*

Henry David Thoreau said, "A man's interest in a single bluebird is worth more than a complete but dry list of the fauna and flora of a town." LARRY DITTO / KAC PRODUCTIONS

LEFT: *This brown pelican has its wings spread on a cool winter day.* GREG LASLEY / KAC PRODUCTIONS

RIGHT: This plump little canyon tree frog looks like a toad with its dark-gray body and irregular brown spots. Its explosive call is a single tone that lasts from one to three seconds. Residing along ponds and rocky streams in the Davis Mountains and Big Bend region, the frog feasts on small insects. It retreats underground to stay warm in cold weather. GREG LASLEY / KAC PRODUCTIONS

BELOW: Turkey vulture drinking from a puddle. Vultures are commonly called "buzzards." The buzzard moniker actually originated with the early English settlers, who mistook the birds for the soaring hawks called buzzards in the Old World.

Turkey vultures have red, bare-skinned heads, long tails, and dingy white lining on the underside trailing edges of the spread wings. They appear to bounce on the wind while rocking sideways on wings held at a pronounced dihedral angle.

Vultures are nature's garbage disposers; they eat carrion and rotting vegetable matter. In rural parts of South America, people in villages depend on vultures to clean up their garbage. In urbanized Texas villages, people may not realize their dependence on vultures to clean the roadways of dead animals. DAVE WELLING

Raccoons are handsome creatures, having dark-gray fur and a fuzzy black-and-white ringed tail. They walk on the soles of their feet just as humans do.
KATHY ADAMS CLARK / KAC PRODUCTIONS

The pied-billed grebe has a blotchy, black-and-white bill and a short, stubby tail. The bird's behavior of sinking silently beneath the water, only to surface unexpectedly at another location, may have given someone long ago the brainstorm for a boat we call the submarine. *LARRY DITTO / KAC PRODUCTIONS*

The great egret is a stately wading bird that's common along the Texas coastal regions as well as at inland lakes, ponds, and streams. BILL DRAKER / KAC PRODUCTIONS

LEFT: *Rio Grande leopard frogs are most active from sunset to sunrise.* BILL DRAKER / KAC PRODUCTIONS

BELOW: *Crested caracara feeding on carrion.*
GREG LASLEY / KAC PRODUCTIONS

The green parakeet is actually a parrot species that has populated the Rio Grande Valley more extensively than the better-known red-crowned parrots of the region. LARRY DITTO / KAC PRODUCTIONS

LEFT: *A mouse peeks out from under a bush. Noted Texas naturalist John Tveten says that it is difficult to identify a mouse without seeing its tail.* DAVE WELLING

BELOW: *Were it not such a common backyard bird, the blue jay would be one of the most sought-after birds for bird watchers. Few birds can match the blue jay's plumage for eye-catching color or can surpass its clever behaviors and distinctive vocalizations.*

Blue jays are in the family Corvidae, which includes twenty North American species such as crows, ravens, and magpies. Bluish-colored corvids like the blue jay are unique to the New World. In the Old World, corvids such as jackdaws and rooks are merely black or sooty gray. ROLF NUSSBAUMER / KAC PRODUCTIONS

Brown pelican gliding on the breeze. They can fly low over the surf on a 6- to 7-foot wingspan, cruising with slow wing beats and long glides over the turbulent air created by bow waves. Suddenly, they'll twist and soar straight up in the air 20 to 60 feet, then pull their wings back, extend their necks, and dive spectacularly into the water.

The adult birds in their breeding plumage have silvery gray-brown bodies and a rich mahogany color that runs up the back of their long necks all the way to their napes. Their crowns have golden-yellow feathers that extend slightly down the sides of their necks. Silky white feathers trim the front of their necks, setting off the blend of brown and yellow tones.

It has been heartening to see brown pelicans return to Galveston since the early 1990s. For a long time, they were only a memory. They began to disappear in the 1950s, and by the 1960s there were no brown pelicans in Galveston or anywhere along the Texas coast except for a handful of birds near Brownsville. KATHY ADAMS CLARK / KAC PRODUCTIONS

LEFT: *Ponds on farms and ranches are an important source of water for coyotes and other wildlife.* DAVE WELLING

BELOW: *This aplomado falcon has a silvery blue back and a cinnamon head. Often seen in pairs, aplomado falcons use the nests of other birds instead of building their own. They feed on birds and large insects.*

These endangered falcons once ranged commonly across the southwestern United States but disappeared in the mid-twentieth century.

In an effort to restore the bird to Texas, The Peregrine Fund released 812 captive-bred aplomado falcons in the 1990s at the Laguna Atascosa National Wildlife Refuge, Aransas National Wildlife Refuge, and Matagorda Island among other locations in South Texas. As of the summer of 2003, eighty-seven birds had been born in the wild in Texas. LARRY DITTO / KAC PRODUCTIONS

As birds of the Chihuahuan Desert and surrounding grass-lands of West Texas, scaled quail feed mostly on seeds but do not hesitate to snatch up insects.

In typical fashion, this breeding male is watching out over his harem from a conspicuous perch.
DAVE WELLING

Roseate spoonbills are mistakenly called flamingos by inexperienced observers.
LARRY DITTO / KAC PRODUCTIONS

This nine-banded armadillo is foraging in an open field for its typical diet of beetles, centipedes, and other ground-dwelling invertebrates. DAVE WELLING

Residing in all regions of Texas, northern cardinals often forage in mated pairs. The birds are expanding their range westward into Arizona, probably because of the rise in numbers of backyard birdfeeders. The male has an enlivening song that sounds somewhat like "cheer-cheer-cheer, pretty-pretty-pretty."

Writing about the cardinal, John James Audubon said, "In richness of plumage, elegance of motion, and strength of song, this species surpasses all its kindred in the United States."

BILL DRAKER /
KAC PRODUCTIONS